CONTEMPORARY ENGLISH
LITERACY

Janet Podnecky

CB

CONTEMPORARY BOOKS

a division of NTC/CONTEMPORARY PUBLISHING GROUP
Lincolnwood, Illinois USA

Cover and Interior Design: William Seabright and Associates
Cover Illustration: Regan Dunnick
Interior Illustrations: David Will, Adam Young

Acknowledgments
The author and publisher would like to thank the following people for their help and
contribution to *Contemporary English, Literacy*:
Gretchen Bitterlin, San Diego Community College, San Diego, CA; **Ann De Cruz**;
Greta Grossman, New York Association for New Americans, New York, NY; **Bet
Messmer**, Educational Options, Santa Clara, CA; **Michael Roddy**, Salinas Adult
School, Salinas, CA; **Federico Salas,** North Harris Montgomery County Community
College, Houston, TX; **Terry Shearer**, Houston Community College, Houston, TX.
Special thanks to **Mark Boone.**

ISBN: 0-8092-0695-1
Published by Contemporary Books,
a division of NTC/Contemporary Publishing Group, Inc.
© 1999 NTC/Contemporary Publishing Group, Inc.,
4255 West Touhy Avenue, Lincolnwood (Chicago), Illinois 60646-1975 U.S.A.
890 VL 0 9 8 7 6 5 4 3 2 1

CONTENTS

ABOUT THIS SERIES

PROGRAM COMPONENTS AND PHILOSOPHY

Contemporary English is a five-level interactive topic-based English-as-a-Second-Language series for adult learners ranging from beginning-literacy level to the high-intermediate level. The series includes

- Student Books for classroom use
- Workbooks (Book 1– Book 4) for independent use at home, in the classroom, or in a lab
- Audiocassettes for individual student, classroom, or lab use and
- Teacher's Manuals with reproducible activity masters and unit progress checks for assessment.

These materials were correlated from inception to the California Model Standards for Adult ESL Programs, the MELT Student Performance Levels, and the SCANS (Secretary's Commission on Achieving Necessary Skills) Competencies.

Unique among ESL series, *Contemporary English* presents high-interest topics as a framework for developing a wide variety of language, thinking, and life skills. In addition to focusing on listening, speaking, reading, and writing skills, *Contemporary English* integrates work on language structures; problem-solving, critical thinking, and graphic-literacy skills; and—increasingly important—work related skills.

Contemporary English empowers students to take charge of their learning and to develop strong communication skills for the real world. For example, each unit in Books 1–4 falls under one of the following broad topics: Home and Neighborhood, People and Machines, Employment and Opportunity, Human Relations, Consumer Economics, Community Services, Transportation and Travel, Healthy Living, History and Geography, and Arts and Entertainment. (The lowest-level book *Contemporary English* Literacy, addresses all of these topics except History and Geography, and Arts and Entertainment.) In short, the series addresses topics of interest and concern to adult learners.

Contemporary English presents engaging and meaningful situations that provide a context for grammar structures, listening activities, and an emphasis on the world of work. Within this framework each unit offers a wealth of pair and group activities, often with designated team roles, and frequent individual and group presentations to the class. This approach mirrors the team organization characteristic of today's workplace and reflects the recent influence on education of the Department of Labor's SCANS report.

UNIT STRUCTURE OF BOOKS 1–4

Contemporary English provides a controlled and pre-dictable sequence of instruction and activities. Conveniently for teachers, each page of a unit functions as a self-contained mini-lesson. Each unit is divided into two parts, each of which begins with a **Scene** that presents, in comic-strip format, incidents from the lives of newcomers to the United States or aspects of U.S. culture that students encounter regularly. Lively, humorous, and dramatic, the **Scenes** engage students in the unit topics—usually by presenting typical problems in the lives of average people. A series of discussion questions proceeds from factual comprehension of the **Scene** to personalization and, in Books 3 and 4, problem solving.

After each opening **Scene** comes **Sound Bites**, a focused listening task that includes pre-listening and post-listening work. **Sound Bites** presents target content and language structures through lively conversations and other samples of natural speech, such as telephone answering-machine messages and transportation announcements.

Throughout *Contemporary English*, grammar structures are first contextualized in the **Scenes** and listening activities and then presented, practiced, and applied on follow-up **Spotlight** pages. Appearing two to four times in each unit, the **Spotlight** pages model target structures in contexts related to the unit topic. Special **Spotlight** feature boxes present the target structures schematically and provide brief, straightforward explanations when necessary. Exercises following the structure presentations allow students to manipulate the structures in meaningful contexts, such as stories or real-life situations. **Spotlight** pages usually end with a **Your Turn** and/or **In Your Experience** activity providing communicative application of the new structures.

These last two features, in addition to **Vocabulary Prompts**, occur within the units at the point of need, rather than in a fixed or unvarying part of each unit. **Vocabulary Prompts**, for example, serves to isolate challenging vocabulary before a listening or reading task. **Your Turn**, a follow up to listening, reading, or structure practice, serves as a participatory task. **In Your Experience**, an activity drawing on students' prior knowledge and personal lives, allows learners to personalize the topics and relate them to their own experience.

Listening and speaking skills are developed further in the **Person to Person** activities, which present recorded two-person conversations in natural, colloquial language. Students listen to conversations, practice them, and work in pairs to complete a final open-ended dialogue. Students can then present their new conversations to the class.

Contemporary English helps students develop their reading skills and become motivated readers of English through **Reading for Real**, a page in each unit that provides stimulating authentic or adapted texts. With passages and realia that typically relate directly to the lives of the characters in the **Scenes**, **Reading for Real** includes such real-life documents as a winning job résumé, instructions for office voice mail, biographies of real people, advice from the local police, and listings of music festivals around the country. Follow-up activities (such as **Your Turn** and **In Your Experience**) extend and personalize the reading.

Culture Corner provides further work on reading skills by focusing on the useful inside information about U.S. life that students love. Presented as brief readings typically paired with charts, graphics, or artwork, **Culture Corner** gives students the information they need to adapt to a culture that can often be confusing and difficult to understand. Interactive follow-up activities help students integrate cultural knowledge with their language skills.

Graphic literacy is the focus of **Get Graphic**, a feature that offers practice in reading charts, graphs, diagrams, and time lines—skills that are crucial in the workplace and for preparing for the GED. **Get Graphic** provides high-interest stimuli related to the unit topics and characters while it incorporates or recycles target language structures. A typical feature of this page is a follow-up activity in which learners develop their own simple graphs or charts and share them with partners or groups. The activities on this page help students learn to read, interpret, and use information in a graphic format.

Problem-solving and critical-thinking skills are developed further in **Issues and Answers**. This feature typically presents two opinions—often in direct opposition—in formats such as advice columns or letters to the editor. **Issues and Answers** contains short, humorous texts with views of U.S. life from a variety of perspectives, including those of immigrants and their "cultural advisors"—the experts who help to orient the newcomers as they bridge the gap between their native and adopted countries.

The last page of each unit contains a **Wrap-Up,** a project in which students use a graphic organizer such as a T-chart, a Venn diagram, an idea map, or a timeline to brainstorm and organize ideas and then talk or write in a group. Following **Wrap-Up** is the self-assessment activity **Think About Learning,** a final reflection task that asks students to evaluate the quality of their own learning on the major content points, life skills, and language structures in the unit. Students can thus assess what they have learned and provide feedback to the teacher, all of which helps to build a learner-centered classroom.

ABOUT *CONTEMPORARY ENGLISH* LITERACY

Contemporary English Literacy is geared toward learners at the preliterate and semiliterate levels. Students at this level generally have no knowledge of English, and they may have absolutely no literacy skills. Some students at this level are non-literate in their native languages, other students are from non-literate cultures. and still others are literate in languages that have a non-Roman alphabet. As a result, students who need work at the level of literacy tend to be a diverse group with very diverse needs.

The Literacy level text was designed to overlap with Book 1 to a certain extent, but the beginning of the text treats beginning literacy skills such as letter formation, directionality, copying, tracing, and distinguishing between uppercase and lowercase letters. With mixed-literacy level and beginning level classes, teachers may wish to use Book 1 with certain sections of the Literacy level. Suggestions for use of these levels are provided in the Literacy Teacher's Manual.

The SCANS competencies targeted in *Contemporary English*, Literacy are the Foundation Skills (listening, speaking, reading, writing, and computational skills).

ICONS

Contemporary English uses the following six icons throughout the series:

 Listening—All conversations and other speech samples are recorded on tape.

 Speaking—Students speak with a partner, a group, or the class.

 Reading—Students read a passage, a graphic, or a short text.

 Writing—Students write letters, words, or phrases.

 Critical Thinking—Students perform an activity that requires critical-thinking skills.

 Spotlight—Students complete an exercise that provides practice on the structures presented on the **Spotlight** page. These exercises may require a variety of language skills, but structure practice is the principal focus of the exercise.

UNIT A

Exercise 1: Circle.

L	(L)EFT	POLICE	WALK
T	TOP	LETTER	DATE
I	ICE	APRIL	IN	CLINIC
H	HOT	RIGHT	HOSPITAL

Exercise 2: Write.

L L L _____

T T T _____

I I I _____

H H H _____

Exercise 3: Circle.

E	(E)MPLOYEE	ENTER	EXIT
F	FIRE	OFF	OFFICE
K	KID	BANK	NICKEL
X	X-RAY	EXIT	TAXI

Exercise 4: Write.

E E E _____

F F F _____

K K K _____

X X X _____

Exercise 5: Circle.

A	(A)GE	NAME	APARTMENT
M	MEN	LIMIT	WOMEN
V	VERY	LIVE	NOVEMBER
N	NO	DON'T	ON	NUMBER

 ## Exercise 6: Write.

A A A _____

M M M _____

V V V _____

N N N _____

Exercise 7: Circle.

C	ⒸLINIC	SCHOOL	CLOSED	
O	OUT	OCTOBER	DOCTOR	
U	UP	TURN	SUNDAY	U.S.A.
G	GO	AGE	GAS	EGGS

 Exercise 8: Write.

C C C _____

O O O _____

U U U _____

G G G _____

Exercise 9: Circle.

S	⒮TOP	PASSING	STATE
D	DON'T	ADDRESS	DOCTOR
P	PARK	UP	OPEN
B	BUS	JOB	BIRTH
R	READ	LIBRARY	RIGHT

Exercise 10: Write.

S S S _____

D D D _____

P P P _____

B B B _____

R R R _____

Exercise 11: Circle.

Q	ⓆUIET	EQUAL	QUARTER
J	JUNE	JOB	JUICE
W	WALK	SAW	WEEK
Y	YEAR	DAY	YES
Z	ZIP CODE	SIZE	ZONE

 Exercise 12: Write.

Q Q Q _____

J J J _____

W W W _____

Y Y Y _____

Z Z Z _____

Exercise 13: Write.

UP ↑

DOWN ↓

_____

_____

STOP

EXIT

_____

_____

MEN

WOMEN

_____

_____

WALK

DON'T WALK

_____

_____

Exercise 14: Write.

ON

OFF

_____

_____

PULL

PUSH

_____

_____

PHONE

CLOSED

_____

_____

HOSPITAL

SCHOOL

_____

_____

UNIT B

Exercise 1: Look. Write. Say.

Aa	Bb	Cc
Dd	Ee	Ff
Gg	Hh	Ii
Jj	Kk	Ll

Mm	Nn	Oo
Pp	Qq	Rr
Ss	Tt	Uu
Vv	Ww	Xx
Yy	Zz	

Exercise 2: Circle.

N	a	h	(n)
P	p	g	r
F	t	b	f
L	k	l	i
A	u	a	c
H	h	m	d
R	e	r	k

Exercise 3: Match.

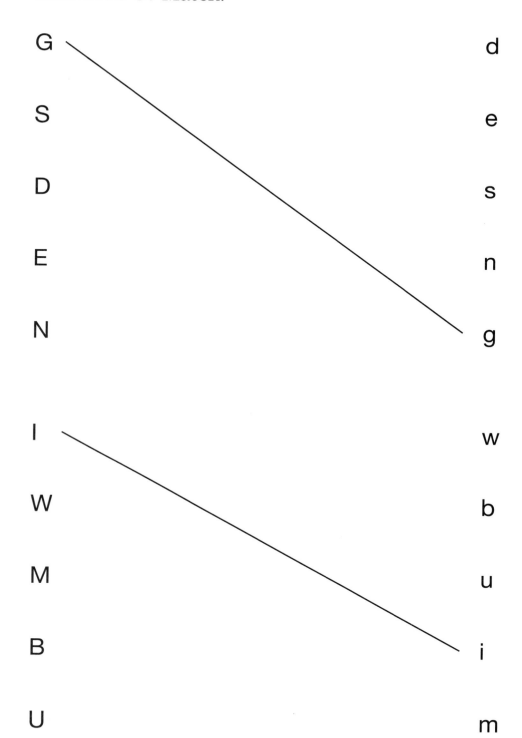

G   d

S   e

D   s

E   n

N   g

I   w

W   b

M   u

B   i

U   m

Exercise 4: Look. Write.

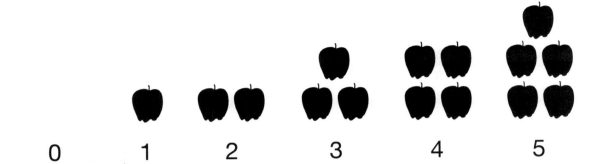

| 0 | 1 | 2 | 3 | 4 | 5 |

0 O O _____

1 1 1 _____

2 2 2 _____

3 3 3 _____

4 4 4 _____

5 5 5 _____

Exercise 5: Look. Write.

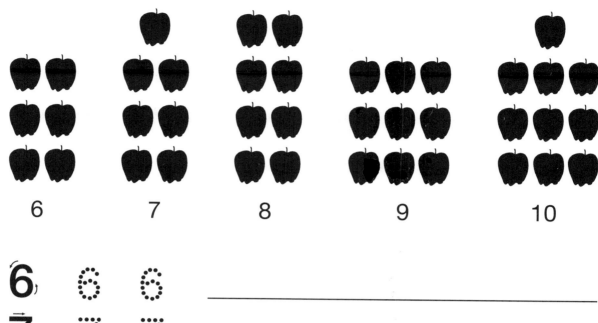

| 6 | 7 | 8 | 9 | 10 |

6 6 6 _____

7 7 7 _____

8 8 8 _____

9 9 9 _____

10 10 10 _____

Exercise 6: Circle.

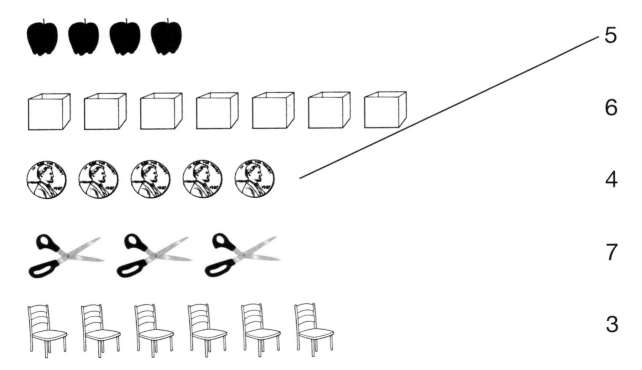

8	
5	
2	
4	
10	

Exercise 7: Match.

5

6

4

7

3

Exercise 8: Write.

   5

   ___

   ___

                                                                   ___

                                                                   ___

                                                                   ___

 **Exercise 9:** Write.

__ 2 3 __ 5 6 __ 8 __

1 __ 3 4 __ __ 7 __ __ 10

— — — — — — — — — — — —

UNIT 1 WHAT'S YOUR NAME?

SPOTLIGHT

Look.

 ## SOUND BITES

Exercise 1: Listen. Point.

YOUR TURN

 Listen. Repeat.

MARC: Hi. I'm <u>Marc</u>.
          What's your name?
SONIA: My name is <u>Sonia</u>.
MARC: Nice to meet you.
SONIA: And you.

Practice with a partner. Use your name.

READING FOR REAL

My first name is Kim. My last name is Lee.

Kim Lee

My first name is Bill. My last name is Miller.

Bill Miller

NAME <u>Kim   Lee</u>
       First   Last

NAME <u>Miller   Bill</u>
       Last   First

Exercise 2: Circle.

1. NAME	NAM	⟨NAME⟩	MANE
2. FIRST	FIRST	FROST	TOAST
3. LAST	LOST	LEFT	LAST
4. Name	Name	Nose	Home
5. First	Fist	First	List
6. Last	East	Last	Late

Exercise 3: Match.

1. Name   Kim <u>Lee</u>

2. First Name   <u>Kim</u> Lee

3. Last Name   <u>Kim</u> Lee

4. Name   <u>Bill</u> Miller

5. First Name   Bill <u>Miller</u>

6. Last Name   <u>Bill Miller</u>

SOUND BITES

 Exercise 4: Listen. Circle. Write.

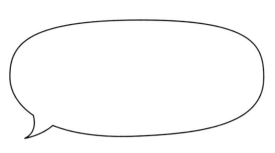

1. (B) T   __B__ ill

2. P   M   ___ arc

3. L   S   ___ ee

4. D   W   ___ avis

5. N   K   ___ im

6. I   A   ___ nna

  ## IN YOUR EXPERIENCE

My first name is Bill. B-I-L-L. My last name is Miller. M-I-L-L-E-R.

Spell your first name.
Spell your last name.

SOUND BITES

Exercise 5: Listen. Circle.

MEN	WOMEN

1.

2.

3.

4.

5. MEN   WOMEN

6. WOMEN   MEN

7. MEN   WOMEN

8. WOMEN   MEN

YOUR TURN

Exercise 6: Match.

1. MEN   2. WOMEN   3. WOMEN   4. MEN

Exercise 7: Write.

Marc Sedar

NAME _____
            First   Last

Sonia Otis

NAME _____
            First   Last

Kim Lee

NAME _____
            First   Last

  IN YOUR EXPERIENCE

What's your name? Write it.

NAME _____
            First   Last

NAME _____
            First   Last

SOUND BITES

Exercise 8: Listen. Circle.

1. Last   (Name)

2. First   Last

3. Last   First

4. First   Name

5. Last   First

6. Last   First

 ## IN YOUR EXPERIENCE

Write.

My name is _____ .

My first name is _____ .

My last name is _____ .

SOUND BITES

Exercise 9: Listen and circle.

1. (Ken)   Pen   Ten

2. Take   Lake   Make

3. Peter   Sedar   Pedro

4. Sale   Pole   Nole

5. Han   Can   Dan

6. Eden   Adams   Odell

YOUR TURN

Copy.

Sonia Otis   Marc Sedar   Anna Davis   Kim Lee   Bill Miller

WOMEN   MEN

Kim Lee   Bill Miller

_____   _____

_____   _____

Write your name. _____

Unit 2   Numbers

Spotlight

Look.

 ## Sound Bites

Exercise 1: Listen. Point.

YOUR TURN

Listen. Repeat.

What's your phone number?

731-4289

Practice with a partner. Use your phone number.

READING FOR REAL

My name is Kim Lee.
My phone number is
234-5521.

My name is Bill Miller.
My phone number is
521-7890.

NAME __Kim_____Lee_____
　　　　　First　　　　　　　Last

PHONE NUMBER
234-5521_____

NAME __Miller_____Bill_____
　　　　　Last　　　　　　　First

PHONE NUMBER
521-7890_____

Exercise 2: Circle.

1. 123	312	⬭123⬭	132
2. 534	533	453	534
3. 748	748	749	148
4. 963	693	963	968
5. 502	802	582	502
6. 841	841	847	341

 Exercise 3: Match.

1. Phone Number   Kim Lee

2. Name   234-5521

3. Last Name   <u>Bill</u> Biller

4. First Name   Bill <u>Miller</u>

SOUND BITES

Exercise 4: Listen. Circle.

1. (742-8901)   724-8801

2. 547-9695   527-6685

3. 321-7474   321-4474

4. 695-4312   965-4421

5. 827-3355   927-3255

6. 278-9110   378-9110

  Exercise 5: Listen. Write.

1. 3 ___ 2- ___ 5 ___ 9   4. 7 ___ ___ -___ ___ 55

2. ___ 31- ___ 46___   5. ___ ___ ___ -4357

3. 8 ___ ___ -032 ___   6. 452- ___ ___ ___ ___

 ## PERSON TO PERSON

ANNA: What's your phone
number?
BILL: 742-8901.
ANNA: 742-8901?
BILL: Yes. That's right.

What's your phone number?

SOUND BITES

Exercise 6: Look. Listen.

11 12 13 14 15 16 17 18 19 20

Exercise 7: Listen. Circle.

1.	12	(15)	18
2.	14	19	13
3.	16	11	20
4.	17	13	19
5.	18	12	16

 ## YOUR TURN

Exercise 8: Match.

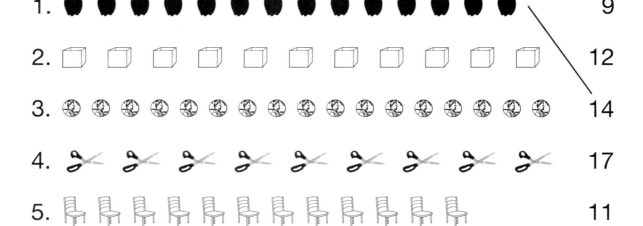

Exercise 9: Write.

1 2 3 4 5 6 7 8 9 10
11 12 13 14 15 16 17 18 19 20

1 ___ 3 4 ___ 6 7 ___ 9 10

___ 12 13 ___ 15 ___ 17 18 ___ ___

<u>1</u> ___ ___ ___ ___ ___ ___ ___ ___ <u>10</u>

<u>11</u> ___ ___ ___ ___ ___ ___ ___ ___ <u>20</u>

1. <u>13</u>

2. ___

3. ___

4. ___

5. ___

6. ___

SOUND BITES

Exercise 10: Listen. Match.

1.

912-7792

212-6764

448-9595

346-4908

384-7210

4.

2.

5.

3.

 # IN YOUR EXPERIENCE

Write.

NAME _____
        Last   First

PHONE NUMBER _____

SOUND BITES

Exercise 11: Listen. Circle.

1.   18   (13)   12

2.   14   11   19

3.   12   15   17

4.   19   16   13

5.   15   14   12

6.   16   17   11

 ## IN YOUR EXPERIENCE

Write.

IMPORTANT PHONE NUMBERS	
NAME	**PHONE NUMBER**
FIRE	
AMBULANCE	
SCHOOL	

UNIT 3 HOME

SPOTLIGHT

Look.

 ## SOUND BITES

Exercise 1: Listen. Point.

YOUR TURN

 Listen. Repeat.

What's your address?

114 Pine Street.

Practice with a partner. Use your address.

READING FOR REAL

NAME ___ Kim ___ Lee ___
First   Last

ADDRESS ___ 802 ___ South Avenue ___
Number   Street

Portland,   OR   97220
City   State ZIP Code

NAME ___ Bill ___ Miller ___
First   Last

ADDRESS ___ 16 ___ Main Street Apt. 4 ___
Number   Street

Somerville, MA   02145
City   State ZIP Code

Exercise 2: Circle.

1. ADDRESS	DRESS	(ADDRESS)	APRIL
2. STREET	STATE	TREAT	STREET
3. CITY	CITY	SIGN	CANDY
4. STATE	STATE	TASTE	STEAK
5. ZIP CODE	ZONE	ZIP CODE	ZERO
6. NUMBER	NUMBER	MEMBER	NAME

Exercise 3: Match.

Address   Street

Sonia Otis

310 Green Street

City   ZIP Code

San Jose, CA 95124

Name   State

SOUND BITES

Exercise 4: Listen. Circle.

1. (Address)   Street   City

2. ZIP Code   State   Number

3. Street   Name   Phone

4. City   ZIP Code   Address

5. Phone   Street   City

6. Name   Number   ZIP Code

 ## PERSON TO PERSON

A: What's your address?
B: 16 Main Street.
A: City and state?
B: San Jose, California.
A: What's your ZIP code?
B: 95124

What's your address? Ask a friend.

SOUND BITES

Exercise 5: Look. Listen.

window   door   book

table   chair   pen

 Exercise 6: Listen. Circle.

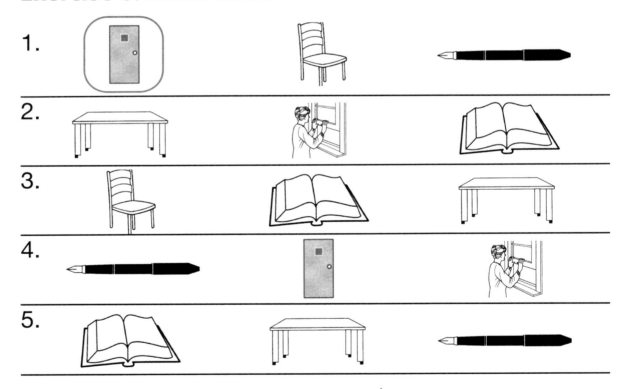

1.

2.

3.

4.

5.

 ## YOUR TURN

Exercise 7: Match.

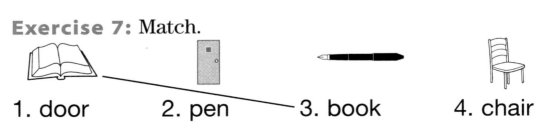

1. door   2. pen   3. book   4. chair

Exercise 8: Count. Write the number.

tables	4
windows	
doors	
books	

SOUND BITES

 Exercise 9: Listen. Circle. Match.

1. (NAME)	NUMBER	A. 520 Park Street
2. BOX	PHONE	B. Denver
3. APPLE	ADDRESS	C. 06321
4. CITY	SLOW	D. Sonia Otis
5. ZOO	ZIP CODE	E. 384-7210

IN YOUR EXPERIENCE

Write.

NAME _____
        First   Last

ADDRESS _____
        Number   Street

_____
      City   State   ZIP Code

PHONE NUMBER _____

SOUND BITES

Exercise 10: Listen. Circle.

1. (818 South Street)   713-6214

2. Somerville   04756

3. Kim Lee   MA

4. 713-6214   Somerville

5. 04756   818 South Street

6. MA   Kim Lee

YOUR TURN

Ask some friends. Write.

ADDRESSES	
NAME	ADDRESS
1.	
2.	
3.	

UNIT 4 LEFT OR RIGHT?

SPOTLIGHT

Look.

 ## SOUND BITES

Exercise 1: Listen. Point.

YOUR TURN

Listen. Repeat.

Where's the bank?

It's on Green Street.

Practice with a partner. Use these places.

hospital

police station

bank

READING FOR REAL

LEFT

RIGHT

The store is on Green Street.
It's **on the left.**

The post office is on Green Street.
It's **on the right.**

Exercise 2: Circle.

1. BANK	FIRST CITY ⬭BANK⬭ AND TRUST
2. STORE	D & R FOOD STORE
3. POST OFFICE	U.S. POST OFFICE HARTLAND 05052
4. LIBRARY	HARTLAND PUBLIC LIBRARY
5. HOSPITAL	SPRINGFIELD HOSPITAL
6. SCHOOL	RIVERSIDE HIGH SCHOOL

Exercise 3: Match.

1. LIBRARY

2. BANK

3. STORE

4. POST OFFICE

5. HOSPITAL

SOUND BITES

  Exercise 4: Listen. Write.

1. BANK

2. STORE

3. HOSPITAL

4. LIBRARY

  ## YOUR TURN

Where's the bank?

It's on the right.

Practice with the other places.

SOUND BITES

Exercise 5: Look. Listen.

1	2	3	4	5	6	7	8	9	10
11	12	13	14	15	16	17	18	19	20
21	22	23	24	25	26	27	28	29	30

 Exercise 6: Listen. Circle.

1.   25   (27)   20

_____

2.   29   19   21

_____

3.   15   22   24

_____

4.   28   18   23

_____

5.   16   26   29

_____

 ## YOUR TURN

Exercise 7: Match.

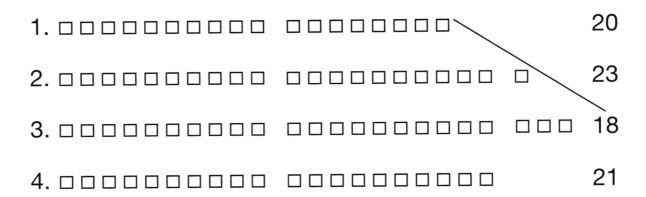

Exercise 8: Write.

A.

1	2	3				
	9	10				
					20	21
			25			
	30					

B.

	EXIT	
Room 21		Room 22
Room 23		Room _24_
Room ___		Room ___
Room ___		Room ___
Room ___		Room 30

SOUND BITES

Exercise 9: Listen. Circle.

1.   bank   

2.   hospital   police station

3.   bank

4. police station   hospital

YOUR TURN

office	left	right
Green	bank	Street

The post _____ is on Green Street. It's on the
_____. The store is on _____ Street. It's
on the _____. The _____ is on Green
_____. It's on the left.

SOUND BITES

Exercise 10: Listen. Circle.

1. (28 Main Street)   25 Main Street

2. 321 Green Street   324 Green Street

3. 729 River Road   722 River Road

4. 520 Adams Avenue   512 Adams Avenue

5. 623 Hope Drive   629 Hope Drive

IN YOUR EXPERIENCE

Write.

Place	Address	Phone Number
School		
Post Office		
Hospital		
Library		

UNIT 5 IT'S TIME

SPOTLIGHT

Look.

SOUND BITES

Exercise 1: Listen and point.

Exercise 2: Listen and repeat.

YOUR TURN

Listen. Repeat.

A: Excuse me,
   what time is it?
B: It's 10:00.
A: Thanks.
B: You're welcome.

Practice with a partner. Use these times.

READING FOR REAL

Shop & Save

STORE HOURS
OPEN   CLOSED
7:00 — 6:00

First City Bank

OPEN 7:00–6:00 Mon.–Fri.
CLOSED Sat./Sun.

Exercise 3: Circle.

1.	1:00	3:00	(7:00)
2.	10:00	3:00	2:00
3.	12:00	6:00	1:00
4.	11:00	5:00	8:00

Exercise 4: Match.

1. 2. 3. 4. 5.

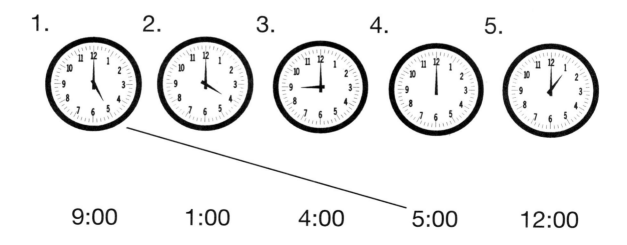

9:00   1:00   4:00   5:00   12:00

Exercise 5: Write.

OPEN

CLOSED

BANK
OPEN _____
CLOSED _____

OPEN

CLOSED

STORE
OPEN _____
CLOSED _____

OPEN

CLOSED

WILSON LIBRARY
OPEN _____
CLOSED _____

PERSON TO PERSON

A: What time does the <u>bank</u> open?
B: <u>9:00</u>.
A: Thank you.
B: You're welcome.

Bank: 9:00–4:00

Practice with a partner.

Post Office: 7:00–5:00

Store: 8:00–8:00

 ## READING FOR REAL

U.S. POST OFFICE Hartland OPEN 8:00–5:00	EVERETT PUBLIC LIBRARY OPEN 10:00–7:00

1. The post office opens at _____.

2. The library opens at _____.

3. The post office closes at _____.

4. The library closes at _____.

SPOTLIGHT ON NUMBERS

Look.

31 32 33 34 35 36 37 38 39 40
41 42 43   50
51   60

 ## SOUND BITES

Exercise 6: Listen. Circle.

1. (34)   37   42   5.   28   38   18

2. 51   60   46   6.   40   34   47

3. 48   39   52   7.   53   35   39

4. 35   25   45   8.   15   50   55

 Exercise 7: Listen. Write.

1. _____   4. _____

2. _____   5. _____

3. _____   6. _____

 ## YOUR TURN

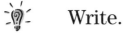 Write.

1. 31 ____ 33 34 ____   3. 54 ____ 56____ 58

2. 46 47 ____ 49 ____

SOUND BITES

Exercise 8: Listen. Write the times.

1.

State Savings Bank
OPEN _____
CLOSED _____

2.

Elm Street Libary
OPEN _____
CLOSED _____

3.

U.S. Post Office
OPEN _____
CLOSED _____

4.

Save More Store
OPEN _____
CLOSED _____

IN YOUR EXPERIENCE

Write the times.

_____   _____

📖 CULTURE CORNER

Look. Read.

7:00 A.M.

8:00 P.M.

Unit 6   My Family

Spotlight

Look.

 ## Sound Bites

Exercise 1: Listen and point.

Exercise 2: Listen and repeat.

YOUR TURN

Listen. Repeat.

A: This is my family.
B: Who's that?
A: That's my <u>daughter</u>.
B: <u>Her</u> name is <u>Mary</u>.

Daughter
Mary

Son
Tom

Practice with a partner. Talk about your family.

READING FOR REAL

FAMILY INFORMATION FORM

NAME ___ Kim ___ Lee ___
First   Last

FAMILY MEMBERS

	NAME	AGE	RELATIONSHIP
SPOUSE	Hung-Ju Lee	42	husband/wife
CHILDREN	Mary Lee	8	daughter
	Tom Lee	7	son

Exercise 3: Circle.

1. CHILDREN	CHICKEN (CHILDREN) CHILLY
2. HUSBAND	HUNGRY HUNDRED HUSBAND
3. WIFE	WIFE WOMEN WISE
4. SON	SAME SON SIGN
5. DAUGHTER	DAWN DAUGHTER BOUGHT

 Exercise 4: Match.

1. family

2. husband

3. son

4. daughter

5. wife

6. children

IN YOUR EXPERIENCE

Write.

My Family

FAMILY INFORMATION FORM

NAME _____
First   Last

FAMILY MEMBERS

NAME   AGE   RELATIONSHIP

_____

_____

_____

PERSON TO PERSON

Listen. Practice with a friend.

A: Is this your <u>brother</u>?
B: Yes, it is.
A: How old is <u>he</u>?
B: <u>He's</u> 22.

READING FOR REAL

FAMILY INFORMATION FORM		

NAME ___Marc___ ___Sedar___ AGE ___26___
     First   Last

FAMILY MEMBERS

NAME	AGE	RELATIONSHIP
Raymond Sedar	52	father
Marie Sedar	50	mother
Tomas Sedar	17	brother
Nancy Sedar	15	sister

1. Who is Marc's father? _____.

2. Who is his mother? _____.

3. How old is Nancy? _____.

4. How old is his brother? _____.

SPOTLIGHT ON NUMBERS

Look.

10 20 30 40 50 60 70 80 90 100

SOUND BITES

Exercise 5: Listen. Circle.

1.	60	(70)	50	5.	83	88	82
2.	75	35	45	6.	72	76	79
3.	58	78	28	7.	67	65	63
4.	31	41	81	8.	91	94	97

Exercise 6: Listen. Write.

1. _____   4. _____

2. _____   5. _____

3. _____   6. _____

YOUR TURN

Write.

81 ____ ____ 84 ____ ____ ____

75 76____ ____ 79 ____ 81

10 20 ____ 40 ____ 60 ____ ____ ____ 100

SOUND BITES

Exercise 7: Listen.

Circle the correct information.

FAMILY INFORMATION FORM

NAME ___ Bill ___ Miller ___   AGE ___ 34/44 ___
          First   Last

FAMILY MEMBERS

	NAME	AGE	RELATIONSHIP
SPOUSE	Susan Miller	42/52	husband /wife
CHILDREN	David Miller	6/16	daughter/son
	Linda Miller	10/12	daughter/son

YOUR TURN

Ask a partner.

Example   A: Who is that?
               B: John.
               A: How old is he?
               B: He's 35.

 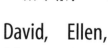

David, Ellen,
32   29

Student A

Name _____   Name _____

Age ____   Age ____

Student B

Bill,   Judy,
28   30

Name _____   Name _____

Age ____   Age ____

 ## CULTURE CORNER

The Nelson Family

NAME	RELATIONSHIP	
Paul Nelson	husband	Mr. Nelson
Denise Nelson	wife	Mrs. or Ms. Nelson

The Timmons Family

NAME	RELATIONSHIP	
Lou Timmons	husband	Mr. Timmons
Cathy Timmons	wife	Mrs. (or Ms.) Timmons
Stan Timmons	son	Mr. Timmons
Ellen Timmons	daughter	Miss or Ms. Timmons

UNIT 7 JOBS

SPOTLIGHT

Look.

 ## SOUND BITES

Exercise 1: Listen and point.

Exercise 2: Listen and repeat.

YOUR TURN

Listen. Repeat.

A: I need a job.
B: What do you do?
A: I'm a <u>cook</u>.
B: Look. Here's an ad
for a <u>cook</u>.

Practice with a partner. Talk about these jobs.

driver

painter

dishwasher

READING FOR REAL

Exercise 3: Circle the jobs. Underline the times.
Circle the phone numbers.

HELP WANTED

Painter	Dishwasher needed	Driver wanted
Mornings	Evenings	Afternoons
8:00 A.M.–12:00 P.M.	5:00 P.M.–10:00 P.M.	2:00 P.M.–6:00 P.M.
Call 655-9275	Call 422-5533	Call 479-8110

Exercise 4: Circle.

1. PAINTER	Wanted: Full-time (painter) for house painting.
2. CASHIER	Opening for cashier. No experience needed.
3. COOK	Experienced line cook for busy restaurant.
4. DRIVER	Delivery driver. Must have good driving record.
5. DISHWASHER	Immediate opening for dishwasher. Flexible hours.

 Exercise 5: Match.

1. painter

2. driver

3. cashier

4. dishwasher

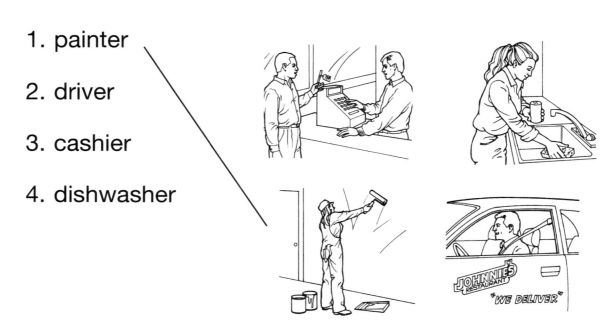

YOUR TURN

Write the jobs.

| dishwasher | cashier | painter |

He's a _____. She's a _____.

She's a _____.

 ## IN YOUR EXPERIENCE

 What do you do? Complete the form.

FAMILY INFORMATION FORM

NAME _____

ADDRESS _____

_____

PHONE NUMBER _____

JOB TITLE _____

PERSON TO PERSON

A: What do you do?
B: I am a <u>driver</u>.
What do you do?
A: I'm a <u>painter</u>.

Listen. Practice with a friend.

READING FOR REAL

JOB APPLICATION

NAME ___Marc___ ___Sedar___ AGE ___26___

ADDRESS ___155 West Street___ PHONE ___437-5561___

___Somerville, MA   02115___

WORK EXPERIENCE

Job Title	Dates	Employer
Cashier	1995–now	Mill Cafe
Cook	1992–1995	Amelia's Restaurant

1. What does Marc do now? He's a _____.

2. Where does he work now? At _____.

SOUND BITES

Exercise 6: Listen. Circle.

1.	1982	(1980)	1922	5.	1919	1991	1908
2.	1993	1939	1930	6.	1981	1971	1961
3.	1975	1965	1995	7.	1963	1986	1946
4.	1998	1988	1990	8.	1985	1955	1975

 Exercise 7: Listen. Write.

1. _____   4. _____

2. _____   5. _____

3. _____   6. _____

 ## YOUR TURN

Write.

    1993–1997   472-6632   317

JOB APPLICATION

NAME __Sonia   Otis__   PHONE _____

ADDRESS _____ Garden Avenue   Boston, MA

WORK EXPERIENCE
Job Title   Dates   Employer

Painter   Steven's Paint Co.

SOUND BITES

Exercise 8: Listen. Circle the correct information.

JOB APPLICATION

NAME <u>Marc Sedar</u> PHONE <u>437-5561/437-6615</u>

ADDRESS <u>155 West Street</u>

<u>Somerville, MA 02115</u>

WORK EXPERIENCE

Job Title	Dates	Employer
Painter/ dishwasher	1995–now	Mill Cafe
Cook/cashier	1992–1995/ 1990–1996	Amelia's Restaurant

 ## YOUR TURN

Ask a partner.

Example: A: What's your name?
        B: <u>John Smith</u>.
        A: What do you do?
        B: I'm a <u>driver</u>.

CULTURE CORNER

 Exercise 9: Write the jobs in the chart. Add other jobs you know.

| painter | cook | cashier | driver |

Jobs in my country	Jobs in the U.S.
cook	cook

 Exercise 10: These are signs at work. Match the signs and the words.

_____ NO SMOKING

_____ FLAMMABLE

_____ POISON

_____ HIGH VOLTAGE

_____ FIRE EXTINGUISHER

a.

b.

c.

d.

e.

UNIT 8 MONEY

SPOTLIGHT

Look.

1¢ 5¢ 10¢ 25¢
$.01 $.05 $.10 $.25

$1
$1.00

$5
$5.00

$10
$10.00

$20
$20.00

  ## SOUND BITES

Exercise 1: Listen and point.

Exercise 2: Listen and repeat.

YOUR TURN

Listen. Repeat.

A: How much is this?
B: 75¢.
A: Thanks.
B: You're welcome.

Practice with a partner. Talk about these prices.

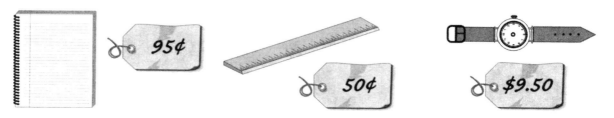

95¢   50¢ $9.50

 # READING FOR REAL

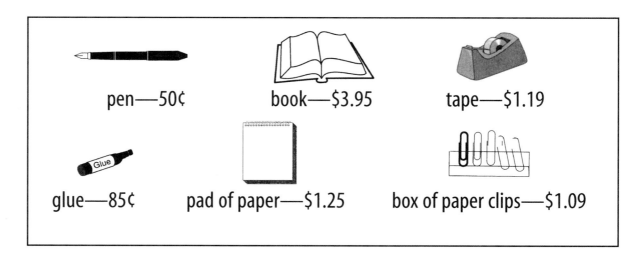

pen—50¢   book—$3.95   tape—$1.19

glue—85¢   pad of paper—$1.25   box of paper clips—$1.09

Exercise 3: Circle.

1.		($1.25) $1.50 $2.25
2.		$4.20 $2.10 $2.40
3.		$5.75 $5.25 $5.50
4.		$3.15 $3.40 $3.60

Exercise 4: Match.

1. $5.75

2. $1.35

3. $2.40

4. $12.50

YOUR TURN

Exercise 5: How much is it? Write.

1. ___$6.75___

2. _____

3. _____

4. _____

Exercise 6: How much is it? Write.

1. 50¢ + 25¢ = ___75¢___

2. 75¢ + 10¢ = _____

3. $2.00 + $3.00 = _____

4. $4.00 + 55¢ = _____

5. $1.00  − 25¢ = ___75¢___

6. $1.00 − 50¢ = _____

7. $2.00 − 75¢ = _____

8. $5.00 − $1.50 = _____

PERSON TO PERSON

Listen. Practice with a friend.

A: How much is it?
B: That's $3.00.
A: Here's $5.00.
B: $2.00 is your change.
A: Thank you.

READING FOR REAL

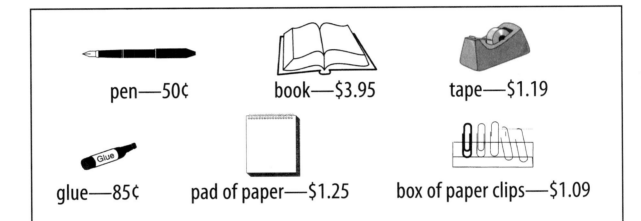

pen—50¢   book—$3.95   tape—$1.19

glue—85¢   pad of paper—$1.25   box of paper clips—$1.09

1. How much is [notepad] ? $1.25

2. How much is [notepad] + [pen] ? _____

3. How much are  ? _____

4. How much are  ? _____

5. How much are +  ? _____

SOUND BITES

  Exercise 7: Listen. Circle.

1. $3.85 ($3.80) $3.15   5. $11.40 $17.40 $11.70

2. $10.60 $7.50 $10.75   6. $23.97 $32.90 $23.79

3. $9.25 $9.95 $5.95   7. $18.10 $14.70 $18.90

4. $3.62 $3.16 $3.92   8. $3.92 $6.50 $15.60

  Exercise 8: Listen. Write

1. _____   4. _____

2. _____   5. _____

3. _____   6. _____

IN YOUR EXPERIENCE

Write.

1. $1.00      4. _____

2. _____   5. _____

3. _____

PERSON TO PERSON

 Listen. Ask a partner.

How much is it?

It's $2.75.

YOUR TURN

 Ask your partner. Write the answers.

Example: B: How much is it?
          A: It's 39¢.

Student A

SALE! SALE!
Low Prices! Great Value!
Office and School Supplies

39¢

$2.25

$1.65

79¢

Student B

Ask your partner. Write the answers.

Example: A: How much is it?
B: It's $1.19.

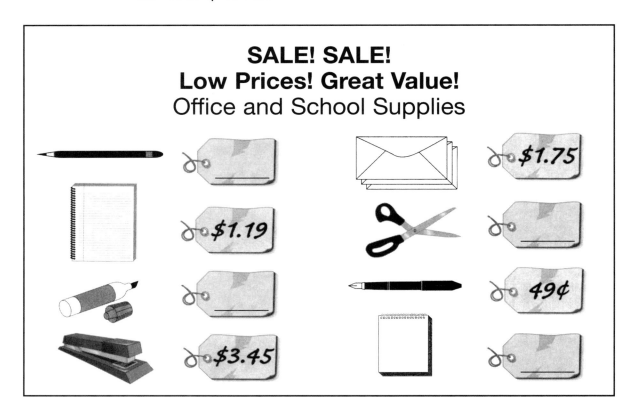

 CULTURE CORNER

That's $24.90. Is that cash or charge?

UNIT 9 LET'S EAT

SPOTLIGHT

Look.

SOUND BITES

Exercise 1: Listen and point.

Exercise 2: Listen and repeat.

YOUR TURN

Listen. Practice with a partner.

A: I need apples.
B: They're in Aisle 1.
A: Thanks.

A: I need fish.
B: It's in Aisle 3.
A: Thanks.

 # READING FOR REAL

SALE! SALE!
Low Prices! Great Value!

$2.49/ 1 bag

49¢/ 1 lb.

69¢/ 1 lb.

$3.75/ 1 lb.

75¢/ 1 head

$3.25/ 1 bag

$1.19/ 1 doz.

89¢/ 1 loaf

Exercise 3: Circle.

1. bread   (eggs)   meat

2. bananas   oranges   apples

3. fruit   lettuce   fish

4. rice   raisins   meat

5. tomatoes   chicken   lettuce

Exercise 4: Circle.

AISLE 1	AISLE 2	AISLE 3
oranges	bread	fish
tomatoes	rice	chicken
bananas		meat

1. (AISLE 1)   AISLE 2   AISLE 3

2. AISLE 1   AISLE 2   AISLE 3

3. AISLE 1   AISLE 2   AISLE 3

4. AISLE 1   AISLE 2   AISLE 3

5. AISLE 1   AISLE 2   AISLE 3

YOUR TURN

Write the prices.

SALE! SALE!
Low Prices! Great Value!

$2.49/ 1 bag

49¢/ 1 lb.

69¢/ 1 lb.

$3.75/ 1 lb.

75¢/ 1 head

$3.25/ 1 bag

$1.19/ 1 doz.

89¢/ 1 loaf

1. oranges $2.49

5. lettuce _____

2. bread _____

6. rice _____

3. eggs _____

7. tomatoes _____

4. fish _____

8. bananas _____

  PERSON TO PERSON

Listen. Practice with a friend.

A: How much is the fish?
B: $3.50 a pound.

A: How much are the eggs?
B: $1.19

READING FOR REAL

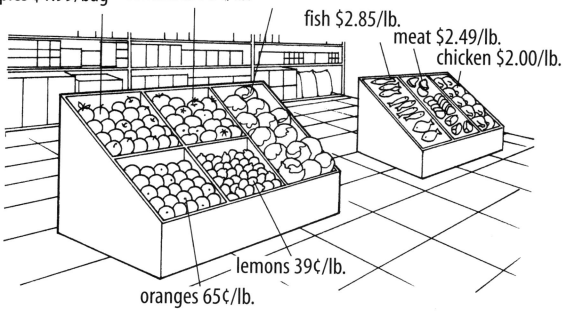

apples $1.99/bag   tomatoes 75¢/lb.   lettuce 99¢

fish $2.85/lb.

meat $2.49/lb.
chicken $2.00/lb.

lemons 39¢/lb.

oranges 65¢/lb.

1. How much is the fish? _____$2.85/lb_____

2. How much are the oranges? _____

3. How much are the tomatoes? _____

4. How much is the chicken? _____

5. How much is the lettuce? _____

6. How much are the apples? _____

7. How much is the meat? _____

SOUND BITES

Exercise 5: Listen. Circle.

1. 89¢ (79¢) 85¢   5. $1.18 $2.80 $1.48

2. $1.15 $1.50 $1.40   6. $2.29 $2.99 $2.19

3. 97¢   57¢   27¢   7. 55¢   65¢   15¢

4. $3.49 $3.39 $4.39   8. $4.09 $4.49 $2.89

Exercise 6: Listen. Write.

1. _____   4. _____

2. _____   5. _____

3. _____   6. _____

IN YOUR EXPERIENCE

How much is it? Write.

1. bread _____   5. lettuce _____

2. bananas _____   6. rice _____

3. eggs _____   7. oranges _____

4. chicken _____   8. tomatoes _____

PERSON TO PERSON

 Listen. Practice with a partner. How much are the eggs?

 ## YOUR TURN

 Ask. Write the prices.

Example: A: How much are eggs?
                B: $1.09

Student A

Shop & Save Super Prices All Week!		
eggs $1.09	bread 65¢	 _____
   _____	apple $1.89	 _____
oranges $2.49	fish $3.25	 _____

Student B

Ask. Write the prices.

Example: B: How much is bread?
          A: 65¢.

Shop & Save Super Prices All Week!		
_____	65¢	tomatoes 95¢
lettuce $1.15	_____	rice $4.80
_____	_____	bananas 39¢

 CULTURE CORNER

Do you have any coupons?

Yes, I do.

| 25¢ OFF | 2 FOR $1.00 |